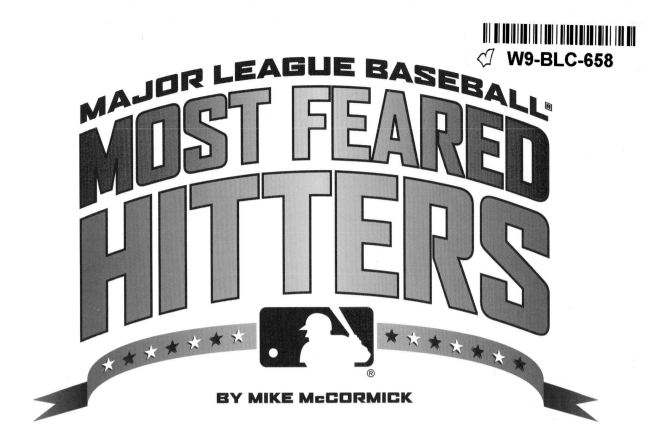

MAJOR LEAGUE BASEBALL®
MOST FEARED HITTERS

BY MIKE McCORMICK

MAJOR LEAGUE BASEBALL® PROPERTIES, INC.

CONTENTS

Major League Baseball: Most Feared Hitters was developed, written and designed by MLB PUBLISHING, the publishing department of Major League Baseball Properties, Inc.
Vice President, Publishing: Donald S. Hintze; Editorial Director: Mike McCormick; Publications Art Director: Faith M. Rittenberg; Senior Production Manager: Claire Walsh; Associate
Art Director: Christina McCormick; Associate Editor: Jon Schwartz; Project Editorial Assistants: Anamika Chakrabarty, Dan Rosen, Nathan Maciborski, Christen D'Alessandro

Printed in the U.S.A.

First Printing: August 2006

ISBN 0-9776476-1-7

PHOTO CREDITS © MLB Photos: John Grieshop (Hafner p. 12, Pujols p. 23); Brad Mangin (Guerrero p. 11, Ramirez p. 19); Rich Pilling (Delgado pp. 4, 6, Rodriguez p. 26); Ron Vesely (Ramirez p. 17, Hafner p. 15); Michael Zagaris (Ortiz p. 18). **© Getty Images:** Stephen Dunn (Guerrero cover/p. 8); Elsa (Pujols cover/p. 20); Otto Greule Jr. (Rodriguez cover/p. 24); Ezra Shaw (Ortiz p. 16). **ILLUSTRATIONS:** Mario Ruiz

IMAGINE YOU'RE A PITCHER in the Major Leagues. You're a confident guy and you've breezed through the first six innings, so you're feeling pretty good about your chances to pick up the victory today. Just as you're settling into a comfort zone, a bloop single and an error put two runners on base with two outs. You figure your stuff is good today so you'll work out of the jam, but then it happens — the opposing team's hulking cleanup hitter strides to the plate. He's clutching a 35-inch tree trunk of a bat like it's a toothpick. You've already gotten him out twice today, but now that there are men on base, everything feels different. Sweat drips down your palm. Your heart thumps in your chest. Your mind races. You check the bullpen, but there's no one out there. It's just you against the big guy. You stare in at the catcher's signs, but none of them look right. What can you throw this guy that he won't airmail to the next zip code?

That's what it's like to face one of the scariest hitters in the Major Leagues. In *Major League Baseball: Most Feared Hitters*, learn everything about these sluggers that you ever wanted to know. Discover where they like the pitch to be thrown, where they hit for the most power, their career home run pace and things they've done that no one else has ever done before. This group has combined for four Most Valuable Player Awards, three batting titles and more than 2,100 career home runs and 6,700 runs batted in. Read on and you'll soon realize why these are the most feared hitters in baseball today.

CARLOS DELGADO

CARLOS DELGADO HAS long been one of the most consistent players in the Major Leagues. While many of the game's best sluggers go through hot and cold streaks, up seasons and down seasons, Delgado remains productive day in and day out. He has hit at least 20 home runs for 10 consecutive years. Of the thousands of Major League players throughout history, just 33 others have accomplished that feat. He also has driven in at least 100 runs in seven out of the last eight seasons. If you want a player who is going to produce runs, Delgado is your man.

"I think Carlos is one of the most feared hitters in the game," says Mets third baseman David Wright. "He has a knack for coming through in RBI situations and he's been one of the best run producers throughout his whole career. He just finds a way to drive in runs."

Delgado can catch fire occasionally, too. In one game during the 2003 season while playing for the Toronto Blue Jays, he became just the 15th player ever to hit four homers in one game. But it's Delgado's everyday impact that benefits his team the most. Many people believe that he is the biggest factor in turning the New York Mets' batting lineup into such a powerhouse in 2006. He brings the rare powerful lefty bat that also can hit for average, which helps balance the lineup. His jovial personality and big shoulders also have taken a huge burden off of other Mets hitters who may have been pressing too hard to perform under pressure. And his knowledge of the game has been very helpful to his teammates.

21

FIRST BASE
NEW YORK METS
BATS: LEFT
THROWS: RIGHT
BORN: 6.25.72
AGUADILLA,
PUERTO RICO

HEAVY HITTER

Delgado likes to swing a big bat. His choice lumber is a whopping 35 inches, 34 ounces, one of the bigger bats in the Major Leagues.

"He really works on pitchers' patterns and stuff like that," says Mets catcher Paul Lo Duca. "He has a great idea of what certain guys are going to throw him. You can really learn a lot from watching him."

Delgado was born in Aguadilla, Puerto Rico, and like many foreign-born ballplayers, he is extremely proud of his heritage. When details for the inaugural World Baseball Classic were announced during the 2005 season, Delgado was one of the first players to jump at the opportunity to represent his homeland. And even though an injury kept him from playing in all but one game, he still sat on the bench rooting for Puerto Rico. "It was quite an honor," he says. "It was a great tournament and we really had a good time."

He grew up in Puerto Rico playing baseball, volleyball and running track, and he loves the island so much that he still lives there during the offseason. In 2001, he had the rare chance to play a Major League game in Puerto Rico when the Blue Jays opened the regular season against the Texas Rangers in San Juan. Those few days proved to be an experience that Delgado never would forget. "It was great," he says. "I was so pumped up in my first at-bat that I had to calm myself down a little bit."

Delgado loved the chance he got to play ball in his homeland, but more importantly, he just loves to play the game every day. For such a big man, he

9

Number of consecutive seasons in which Carlos has walloped at least 30 home runs.

always has been a workhorse for his teams, playing in at least 128 games every year since becoming a full-time Big Leaguer back in 1996. He even achieved "perfect attendance" by playing in all 162 games during the 2000 and '01 seasons. Think about how tough it is to show up to school every day, and that's without facing laser-fast line drives and 98-mph fastballs.

Speaking of the fastball, Delgado is, in one way, like most big sluggers — he absolutely loves to hit them. Through the early part of the 2006 season, his batting average was nearly 100 points higher against fastballs than it was against curveballs. If Delgado had his choice, the pitcher would fire him a nice fastball on the inside half of the plate — that's where he really likes to see a "fat pitch" that he can turn on and crush.

Defenses try some odd tricks when Delgado comes to the plate. Many teams will use what is called a heavy shift against him. Since he loves to pull the ball — which means that, as a left-handed hitter, he normally hits to right field — managers will stack an extra infielder on the right side. It's a pretty funny sight to see. The third baseman will play near short, the shortstop will play closer to where the second baseman usually is positioned, and the second baseman will play a few feet onto the outfield grass in shallow right field. They figure that if Carlos is going to hit it there, the more gloves in that area to catch it, the better the chance to get him out — but that's no easy task!

FEAR FACTOR

Delgado would fit in perfectly in a classroom because he's a great note-taker. If you watch closely, you can see him scribbling into a notebook in the dugout after each at-bat. He marks down how each pitcher tried to get him out so he can know what to expect the next time.

VLADIMIR
GUERRERO

FORMER U.S. PRESIDENT Theodore Roosevelt once said, "Speak softly and carry a big stick." That phrase perfectly describes Vladimir Guerrero. The president, known as "Teddy," was referring to foreign policy, but speaking softly and carrying a very big stick also represents the way in which Guerrero, a superstar outfielder for the Los Angeles Angels of Anaheim, goes about his business as one of the most feared sluggers in Major League Baseball.

People usually refer to him as "Vladi" or "Vlad," and some fans in Anaheim even have taken to the nickname of "Big Daddy." Whatever you call him, Guerrero has become known as the shyest superstar in the Big Leagues today. But don't let his quiet personality fool you. He also has the reputation of swinging a ferocious bat, and that has caused pitchers everywhere to run and hide. He reached 300 career homers before he turned 30 years old, which is a pretty amazing achievement, and his lifetime batting average of .324 entering the 2006 season shows that he's not just a power threat.

Guerrero also has an amazing ability to hit a pitch — and hit it with crushing force — no matter where it's thrown. He just *loves* to swing. Whether the ball is high, low, outside or inside, no pitch is safe when Vlad is up there hacking. He has been known to hit homers on balls that skipped in the dirt. Fans love to watch him reach for balls, but you can be sure that pitchers get frustrated with how hard it is to throw anything past him.

RIGHT FIELD
LOS ANGELES ANGELS
OF ANAHEIM
BATS: RIGHT
THROWS: RIGHT
BORN: 2.9.76
NIZAO,
DOMINICAN REPUBLIC

"There's really no way to pitch to him," says Cardinals shortstop and former teammate David Eckstein. "You throw balls out of the strike zone, and those are the pitches that he crushes."

Guerrero is very proud of his Dominican heritage, and he also is a great family man. He was extremely excited to play for his country in the first World Baseball Classic in 2006, but three of his cousins died in a tragic car accident in the Dominican Republic just before the event started. He decided to skip the Classic so that he could spend time with his family after such a devastating loss.

Vlad always has remained close to his family. In fact, 15 of his relatives live near him in Southern California and there are "too many close relatives to count" in the Dominican village of Nizao, where he is considered a national hero. "I can walk around there like any other human being. But usually I get mobbed on Sunday." When asked why everything changes on Sunday, Vlad replies with his trademark big smile: "They need a little extra cash for the week, so they hit me up for money then."

Just 30 years old, Guerrero has a lot of swings left, but he already has compiled numbers that would make for

The average number of pitches that Vlad sees in each at-bat, among the lowest in the Major Leagues.

a great career. He has finished seven of the last eight seasons with at least 30 home runs, 100 RBI and a batting average of at least .300. When he joined the Angels in 2004, pitchers hoped he would take a year to adjust to the American League. No such luck. He quickly showed his new teammates and opponents that he could single-handedly dominate a game. In one contest that season, he went 4 for 4 at the plate with two roundtrippers and a team-record nine RBI. Angels teammate Darin Erstad says, "We heard a lot about him before he got here, but there's nothing that can prepare you for what he does. He's absolutely amazing. A mega-superstar."

Vlad batted .337 with 39 homers and 126 RBI to win the AL Most Valuable Player Award in 2004. The day that he returned to the Dominican Republic after winning the award was declared a national holiday in his country.

Not one to slow down, Vlad has kept the intense pressure on opposing pitchers ever since then. True to his reputation, he just keeps on smiling and lets his mean, giant stick do the talking.

THE INTIMIDATOR
Some pitchers just won't give Guerrero any chances — Vlad was among his league's top five in intentional walks each season since 1999. He ranked first twice.

TRAVIS HAFNER

TRAVIS HAFNER HAD a backup plan. If he didn't make it to the Big Leagues in baseball, the man with one of the most unique nicknames in the game — Pronk — planned to become a professional wrestler. After all, the Indians' powerful first baseman is a huge fan of the WWE (World Wrestling Entertainment). How could he not be? Hafner is a huge hulk of a man. At 6 feet 3 inches tall and 240 pounds, he's bigger than SmackDown superstar and world heavyweight champion Rey Mysterio, Intercontinental champion Shelton Benjamin and many other star wrestlers of the WWE.

Pitchers already had enough images in their head to scare them out of wanting to face Hafner in the batter's box. Now if they imagine "Pronk the Masked Marauder" leaping from the top of the dugout to deliver an elbow drop, they may never sleep another wink.

At least judging by the competitive nature that he shows on the field, it sure seems like Pronk would have made quite a wrestler. That intense desire to win dates all the way back to his childhood.

"One time when I was pitching in Little League, I gave up some runs," he says. "I was backing up home plate and I threw my glove down. My dad pulled me aside and said, 'You better never do that again.' That straightened me out."

Hafner grew up in a small town called Sykeston, North Dakota — an unusual place for a baseball player to develop because of the harsh weather. Believe it or not, though, he isn't the first Big Leaguer to hail from that area. The Angels' Darin Erstad is from

48

DESIGNATED HITTER
CLEVELAND INDIANS
BATS: LEFT
THROWS: RIGHT
BORN: 6.3.77
SYKESTON,
NORTH DAKOTA

7

The number
of extra-base hits
(doubles, triples
and home runs)
Hafner had in just
12 at-bats during
a pressure-packed
series against
division-rival
Chicago in
September 2005.

nearby Jamestown, so there must be something in the water there that helps produce tough, hard-nosed Major League ballplayers.

Many sports appealed to Hafner when he was young, but he mostly participated in basketball and track. It's no surprise to learn that he was a great discus thrower, but it's shocking to know that he also placed third in the state in the triple jump his senior year. He insists that he wasn't quite as big back then, but seeing that large body jump with that kind of speed must have been some sight! Of course, Hafner also played Little League, Babe Ruth League and American Legion ball as a kid, and that's where he first showed signs of the amazing ability he displays today. "I just enjoyed playing the game," he says. "Baseball was so much fun."

Sykeston was about 380 miles from the nearest Major League park, but Hafner still found ways to live and breathe baseball. "I used to watch Orioles and Braves games on satellite," he says. "My favorite players were Eddie Murray, David Justice and Cal Ripken."

HE'S NO DUMMY

Hafner actually was the valedictorian of his high school class. Out of the eight students graduating in his senior year, Travis had the highest grade-point average of them all — 3.99.

Hafner first burst onto the Major League scene in 2004. Not many people yet knew his name — and definitely not his nickname — but it wasn't long before pitchers around the league were forced to take notice. He batted .311 with 28 homers and 109 RBI that year, a clear sign that Hafner was going to intimidate pitchers for years to come. It's very difficult to defend against Hafner because he hits the ball hard to all fields. He pulls the ball 40 percent of the time, but 28 percent of his hits go to the opposite field.

He swung his way to even greater on-field success in 2005, earning himself a place on the list of elite American League sluggers. In just his second full season, he finished fifth in the AL Most Valuable Player Award voting. When the Indians challenged the White Sox for the division crown in September 2005, Hafner was at his best. He belted 11 home runs in the season's final month, helping his team stay in the pennant race and letting opponents around the league know that "Pronk" swings some heavy lumber.

Which brings us back to his nickname. Hafner's teammates were torn over whether to call him "The Project," because he was a work in progress, or "Donkey," because he was a big guy who, some said, resembled the animal when he ran the bases. Unable to decide, they combined the two ideas to come up with "Pronk." And now that there is a Pronk Bar, which Hafner calls, "The best candy bar you'll ever taste," it's a sure bet that kids around Cleveland won't be able to get enough of their slugging star.

ALL ABOUT LOCATION
Hafner loves to crank pitches that are up in the strike zone. He batted a whopping .391 in 2005 when swinging at pitches that were thrown high and outside.

DAVID

34

DESIGNATED HITTER
BOSTON RED SOX
BATS: LEFT
THROWS: LEFT
BORN: 11.18.75
SANTO DOMINGO,
DOMINICAN REPUBLIC

ORTIZ

MANNY

RAMIREZ

24

LEFT FIELD
BOSTON RED SOX
BATS: RIGHT
THROWS: RIGHT
BORN: 5.30.72
SANTO DOMINGO,
DOMINICAN
REPUBLIC

ORTIZ AND MANNY. Manny and Ortiz. The Boston Red Sox are lucky to have the most powerful pairing in any lineup anywhere. The duo combined for 92 homers and 292 RBI in 2005. No two teammates in the Majors did more damage that season.

To put their power in historical perspective, want to hear what kind of company they keep? Have you heard of Babe Ruth and Lou Gehrig? They may have played a long time ago, but anyone who knows baseball is familiar with their legendary names. Way back in 1930 and '31, Ruth and Gehrig became the only teammates in history with two consecutive seasons in which they both collected 40 home runs and 130 RBI. The only teammates, that is, until Ortiz and Manny achieved the feat in 2004 and '05.

"They're the best one-two punch in baseball," says White Sox bench coach Tim Raines. "They bat in the middle of the lineup and both have more than 100 RBI. It's crazy to see two of those guys in the same lineup. It's really tough to face."

Don't miss one of Ortiz's at-bats late in a game because 19 of his 47 homers in 2005 came in the seventh inning or later. ... Most right-handed hitters like the ball up in the strike zone, but Ramirez has an uncanny ability to rip low pitches.

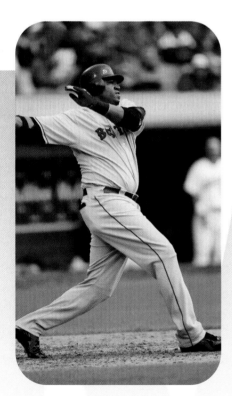

DYNAMIC DUO

There's no way around Boston's one-two punch. How can you walk Big Papi with Manny hitting behind him?

Ortiz goes by the nickname "Big Papi," and at 6 foot 4, 230 pounds, it's easy to see why. While he is the gentlest of giants off the field, pitchers need to beware when the big man confidently strides up to the plate. And when the outcome of the game hangs in the balance, pitchers usually are better off walking him.

Look up the word "clutch" in the dictionary and you may see a photo of Ortiz. In September 2005, the Sox gave him a plaque naming him the "best clutch hitter in franchise history" after he hit his seventh career walk-off homer for Boston. During the team's championship season in 2004, Ortiz launched his biggest hit — a game-winning dinger off Yankees reliever Paul Quantrill in the 12th inning of Game 4 of the ALCS. "He's the last guy you want to see up in a big situation," says former Yankee John Flaherty. In 2005, 19 of Ortiz's 47 home runs either tied a game or gave the Red Sox a lead.

If Ortiz is the thunder, then his partner in crime, Ramirez, is the lightning. Ramirez has one of the quickest bats in baseball. Thanks to that swing, he can watch a pitch longer than most hitters and still catch up to the ball. That makes it easier to recognize what's coming.

Ramirez is the perfect middle-of-the-batting-order teammate for Ortiz. If a pitcher faces the Red Sox, he knows of the great

danger he'll face when Ortiz and Ramirez come up back-to-back. Boston has learned to rely on the mighty bats in the middle of its lineup, and fans have learned to rely on Manny's ability to determine how far the team goes. In 2005, he hit .353 with 36 homers in Red Sox wins. In Boston losses, on the other hand, he batted just .211 with nine home runs.

"I still think the scariest person we face is Manny Ramirez," says Angels first baseman Darin Erstad. "You want to talk about single-handedly taking over a game, I think that he's the kind of guy that can do that."

Watching from a distance, people sometimes think that Ramirez isn't always concentrating. But with the numbers he posts, that's hard to believe. As Ortiz and his teammates will tell you, his approach is just "Manny being Manny." "He doesn't get frustrated," says teammate Matt Clement. "He's so laid back, but he plays the game hard. It's rare."

It's even more rare to find two of the game's most feared sluggers stacked back-to-back in the same lineup. But unfortunately for opposing pitchers, that's exactly what the Red Sox have.

Number of home runs belted by both Ortiz and Ramirez from 2004 to 2005, more than any other player in baseball during those two seasons.

ALBERT PUJOLS

ALBERT PUJOLS IS the best hitter in Major League Baseball today. Just try to dispute the fact — the argument will fall flat. He won the Rookie of the Year Award in 2001, was named the National League MVP in 2005, and every year he's a prime candidate for the Triple Crown, ranking among the league's leaders in batting average, home runs and RBI. While the National League hasn't had a Triple Crown winner since 1937, it certainly hasn't had a pure hitter like Pujols in an extremely long time.

Before Pujols turned 26 years old, he already had posted five seasons with at least 30 HR, 100 RBI and a batting average above .300. He was the first player ever to record those statistics in each of his first five years. He also reached 1,000 career hits and 200 HR faster than any player in Major League history. That's anyone in the *entire* history of the game, including Babe Ruth, Ted Williams, Hank Aaron and everyone else. Pujols achieved those marks in just 806 games. The previous record holder (at 825 games) is a player you've probably heard of, as well: Willie Mays. "Albert is going to the Hall of Fame," says fellow National League slugger Derrek Lee. "He 'struggles' and he still hits .330. He's such a disciplined hitter, and I don't really see any holes with him."

Unfortunately for the pitchers facing Pujols, they don't see any holes in his swing either. Right-handed batters often hit poorly against right-handed pitchers, but not Pujols — Albert batted 40 points higher with 25 more longballs against righties than lefties in 2005. And if a pitcher makes the mistake of

5

FIRST BASE
ST. LOUIS CARDINALS
BATS: RIGHT
THROWS: RIGHT
BORN: 1.16.80
SANTO DOMINGO,
DOMINICAN REPUBLIC

74

Many players believe that Pujols has a good chance to set a new single-season home run record, which would require this number.

throwing a first-pitch ball to Pujols, then he might as well throw in the towel. Pujols hits .398 after getting ahead 1-0.

He might make hitting look so easy, but one of the keys to Albert's success is that he works as hard as he can at it because he realizes it's not easy at all. "Hitting is a tough thing to do," Pujols says. "I try to always show up very early before games. I like to have time to think about everything I want to work on and not get rushed."

One of the ideas that Albert has come up with is using different bats against right-handed and left-handed pitchers. He swings a 33-ounce bat against southpaws, but gains a little more power by using a 34-ounce piece of lumber against righties. He used one of those lucky 34-ouncers to crush one of the most memorable home runs of his career. The Cardinals were facing elimination in Game 5 of the 2005 National League Championship Series against the Houston Astros, who had their nearly perfect reliever, Brad Lidge, on the mound. Trailing by two runs with two outs and no one on in the top of the ninth, the Cardinals kept their season alive when David Eckstein and Jim

FIERCELY FOCUSED

Albert has been known to disappear into the video room after an at-bat to watch his swing and make sure there are no obvious signs of any bad habits.

Edmonds worked their way on base. And that's exactly what you want to do when you're batting in front of Pujols, who crushed a hanging slider 412 feet to lead the Cardinals to a 5-4 victory and a trip back to St. Louis for Game 6. Even though the Cardinals ended up losing the Series, it was one of the most memorable homers in playoff history.

It certainly was Pujols' most notable blast so far, but surely there are more to come. If he continues his pace of averaging 40 longballs per season, Albert has a legitimate chance of challenging Hank Aaron's all-time home run record (755) later in his career. Because his swing is so simple and compact, he's likely to avoid long slumps, so keeping such a terrific pace is very possible. Albert blasted 20 home runs in the Cardinals' first 42 games in 2006. That was the hottest start ever, but then he injured a muscle in his side and was placed on the disabled list. Otherwise, baseball fans may have seen Pujols chase the single-season home run record of 73 dingers, held by Barry Bonds.

When you hear names like "Big Papi" and "Pronk," you realize about the only thing Pujols doesn't have yet is a catchy nickname. In an ESPN poll, voters selected "Winnie the Pujols" over "Phat Albert" as broadcaster Chris Berman's best nickname for Albert. Whatever you call him, Pujols is likely to be remembered for a long time after he stops playing. "Albert is the best player I've ever played with," says Edmonds. "He's going to be one of the best players the game has ever seen."

MAN IN MOTION

Albert relies on rotating his hips to allow him to drive the ball. Coaches say that sluggers need to "get their hips out of the way" before they swing. Albert gets his hips out of the way in a hurry.

ALEX RODRIGUEZ

WHILE ALBERT PUJOLS gains a lot of attention for being the most dangerous hitter in the Major Leagues, Alex Rodriguez has been the best *all-around* player for years. In fact, it's safe to say that anytime the New York Yankees take the field, A-Rod is the greatest talent in the ballpark. He's a perfect example of a "five-tool player": He hits for a high average, he definitely can hit for power, he has great running speed, he's a tremendous fielder, and he has a very strong throwing arm. In other words, he can help his team in many different ways. But it's his bat that strikes the most fear into the hearts of opposing pitchers and managers throughout the league.

"He's a tremendous talent and pitchers know how strong he is," says Yankees teammate Johnny Damon. "He's one of those God-given talent guys who can resemble Hercules."

A career .307 hitter entering 2006, Rodriguez already has won two American League MVP Awards (in 2003 and '05). He has led the league in longballs four times, while also becoming the youngest player ever to reach the 400-home run plateau — he did it at age 29 in 2005. That's a huge reason why Alex may become the career home run king before he retires. If he has one concern about his success at the plate, it's keeping himself from swinging too hard and trying to do too much every time he comes to bat. "I love my swing. I do," says Rodriguez. "But my swing, because I'm such a big guy, really has to be at the right tempo." Alex estimates that his ideal hack is

13

THIRD BASE
NEW YORK YANKEES
BATS: RIGHT
THROWS: RIGHT
BORN: 7.27.75
NEW YORK, NEW YORK

ONE OF THE GUYS

Alex loved collecting baseball cards when he was a kid. At one point, he owned more than 200,000 cards.

with about 70 percent of his strength. He tries to avoid swinging as hard as he can because swinging wildly makes it harder to make good contact with the ball.

A-Rod's super talents on the ballfield were obvious from a young age. In 1993, he was the first high school player ever to try out for Team USA. He also played for the U.S. Junior National Team that summer. He first appeared in the Major Leagues with the Seattle Mariners at the tender age of 18 in 1994. He terrorized pitchers back then, and he only has gotten better since. "I played with him for three years and I know what he's capable of," says Rangers shortstop Michael Young. "New York is just starting to see what he's capable of. He can do more than this. He's just getting his feet wet. He'll only get better."

Getting better isn't exactly the easiest thing when you're already the best. A-Rod's attack is more balanced than any of the other super sluggers in the Major Leagues. He hits for roughly the same average whether he's facing right-handed or left-handed pitchers. He can dominate a game with his power, with base hits, on the bases or while playing

10

Number of runs Rodriguez drove in in one game against the Angels in 2005.

defense. You name it, and A-Rod can do it well. Speed is another area in which Rodriguez excels beyond the other top hitters in the game. And that speed inspires even more fear in pitchers than his bat alone. He has stolen well over 200 bases during his career so far, and at least 15 in each of the past three seasons. While most sluggers get a hit or a walk and stay at first base, Alex can earn a walk and then steal second to get into scoring position. It's almost unfair to pitchers how many ways A-Rod can hurt them.

Pittsburgh Pirates Hall of Famer Honus Wagner earned his place as the greatest hitting shortstop of all time. If A-Rod had not switched positions in 2004 — from shortstop to third base when he joined the Yankees — he certainly would have cemented his own legacy as the greatest shortstop ever. But it was more important for him to move to a team that gave him a better chance to win a World Series. "Honestly," he says, "if I never play another inning at shortstop the rest of my life, I'll be okay. I'm surprised. I thought I would miss it a lot more, but there has not been one time when I thought, 'I wish I was over there.' Even during the couple innings I have played at short for the Yankees, I was like, 'Okay, I want to go back to third.'"

If he stays at his current position, you can bet that A-Rod soon will become known as one of the greatest ever to play third, or as Big Leaguers call it, the "hot corner." But no matter where he plays on the field, he will be known as one of the most complete players of all time.

ON THE RISE

Keep an eye on Alex's career home run total. In his first 12 seasons (through 2005), he tallied 429 career homers. Whether the home run king 10 years from now still is Hank Aaron or it is someone new, Rodriguez is likely to challenge that mark.

OFFENSE

Now that you've read all about what it takes to be a feared slugger in the Major Leagues, you should be keeping an eye on the stat sheets. Below is a grid for you to fill in the leaders in

AMERICAN LEAGUE

PLAYER	SEASON	HOME RUNS	RUNS BATTED IN	BATTING AVERAGE
VLADIMIR GUERRERO				
TRAVIS HAFNER				
DAVID ORTIZ				
MANNY RAMIREZ				
ALEX RODRIGUEZ				

TRACKER

batting average, home runs and RBI in each league. We've already filled in the names of the players in this book for you — now use the blank spaces to track any of your other favorite players.

NATIONAL LEAGUE

PLAYER	SEASON	HOME RUNS	RUNS BATTED IN	BATTING AVERAGE
CARLOS DELGADO				
ALBERT PUJOLS				

FUN & GAMES

Hidden in the grid below are the last names of seven of Major League Baseball's biggest sluggers, plus the nickname for three of them and a few other home run terms we challenge you to locate. The names and words are listed in all different directions: forward, backward, up, down and diagonally. How many can you find?

```
B  A  S  E  C  R  Y  E  I  Z  C  B  O  L  G
D  E  L  S  L  O  J  U  P  S  A  W  D  E  U
R  C  A  R  O  D  L  A  P  C  N  K  A  Z  E
Z  O  A  A  W  R  P  V  G  U  B  A  F  N  R
C  E  D  O  I  I  P  T  O  H  S  N  O  O  M
E  D  V  R  G  G  D  E  L  A  A  Q  C  M  A
T  X  B  A  I  U  U  U  G  F  A  F  D  Y  L
S  L  U  G  G  E  R  E  Z  N  W  E  E  C  S
A  A  M  C  Q  Z  X  A  R  E  O  X  L  S  D
L  K  Z  T  B  O  Z  A  T  R  O  L  G  Y  N
B  Y  N  R  E  S  M  U  T  P  E  Y  A  B  A
B  K  N  O  I  I  Y  I  U  M  B  R  O  Q  R
T  A  Z  P  R  X  Z  N  M  R  E  M  O  H  G
R  D  A  E  Z  P  O  Y  H  D  D  J  V  C  O
U  P  Z  B  X  L  A  J  O  L  B  R  O  D  W
```

A-ROD	GRAND SLAM	HOMER	PAPI	RAMIREZ
BLAST	GUERRERO	MOONSHOT	PRONK	RODRIGUEZ
DELGADO	HAFNER	ORTIZ	PUJOLS	SLUGGER

WHO AM I?

By now you should be very familiar with the names and accomplishments of the seven players featured in this book. So let's see if you've been paying attention. Match the descriptions on the left to the player on the right. Each player will be the answer to just one clue. Use the space we've provided after each clue to fill in the last name of the correct player. And here's a hint: All of the answers can be found somewhere within the pages of this book. Good luck!

1. My hot start in 2006 included 20 homers in my first 42 games. _____
2. I donate 127 tickets to charity for every one of my team's home games. _____
3. My home run in Game 4 of the 2004 ALCS kept my team alive so that we could reach the World Series. _____
4. I go by the nickname "Pronk."_____
5. In 2005, I hit 36 homers in my team's wins. _____
6. I use a big, 35-inch, 34-ounce bat. _____
7. I'm the youngest player ever to reach 400 career home runs. _____

Carlos Delgado

Vladimir Guerrero

Travis Hafner

David Ortiz

Albert Pujols

Manny Ramirez

Alex Rodriguez

HARD-HITTING TRIVIA

Now that you're warmed up with some of the easier games and puzzles, it's time to really test your baseball knowledge. Below are some tough trivia questions about the seven super sluggers featured inside this book. Some of these you might know off the top of your head, but other questions will send you scrolling through team websites or historical books. So get ready to swing for the fences with these stumpers!

1. Where did Carlos Delgado grow up?
2. Which two batting milestones did Albert Pujols reach faster than anyone ever?
3. As a kid, Alex Rodriguez owned 200,000 of these.
4. David Ortiz hit 47 HR in 2005. How many of them tied a game or gave the Red Sox the lead?
5. Manny Ramirez has more than 200 HR as a member of the Red Sox. Who holds Boston's all-time career record for homers?
6. What does Travis Hafner say he'd be doing if he wasn't a pro baseball player?
7. In what category has Vladimir Guerrero ranked in the top 5 every year since 1999?

THE FIRST TIME

A Big League superstar may hit hundreds of home runs during his career, but he'll always remember the first. Match the players in the left column with the date of their very first Major League home run in the right column.

DELGADO	9/3/93
GUERRERO	4/4/94
HAFNER	6/12/95
ORTIZ	9/21/96
PUJOLS	9/14/97
RAMIREZ	4/6/01
RODRIGUEZ	4/17/03

Answers on page 32

FUN & GAMES: ANSWERS

WORD SEARCH

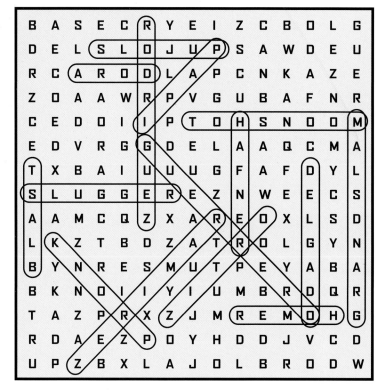

WHO AM I?
1. Pujols
2. Guerrero
3. Ortiz
4. Hafner
5. Ramirez
6. Delgado
7. Rodriguez

HARD-HITTING TRIVIA
1. Puerto Rico
2. 1,000 Hits, 200 HR
3. Baseball cards
4. 19
5. Ted Williams (521 HR)
6. Pro wrestler
7. Intentional walks

THE FIRST TIME
Delgado: 4/4/94
Guerrero: 9/21/96
Hafner: 4/17/03
Ortiz: 9/14/97
Pujols: 4/6/01
Ramirez: 9/3/93
Rodriguez: 6/12/95